And Listen to the Waves

Selected Poems

Brian Churcher

BRAMBLEBY BOOKS

And Listen to the Waves – Selected Poems

A CIP catalogue record for this book is available from the British Library

ISBN 9781908241191
eISBN 9781908241252

Published 2013 by
Brambleby Books Ltd., UK
www.bramblebybooks.co.uk

Cover design by Creatix Design
Cover photo by Hugh Loxdale

Printed and bound by Printondemand-worldwide, UK
FSC and PFSC accredited

And Listen to the Waves

To June,
my little critic!
Brian

To my wife Margaret, daughter Caroline, son Chris, and my friends who have encouraged me, and without whose help I would not have written these poems.

About the Author

Having left my local Grammar School, although I had qualified to go on to University but decided not to, I tried my hand at many other ways of earning a living – from farm work, to Police Officer (several of my ancestors had been high-ranking officers) and, as my father suggested when I seemed to be at a loose end, to becoming a city broker in Lloyds of London, which I did for ten years. Anything, in fact, that seemed interesting at the time and broadened one's outlook and experience of life. For example, I auditioned and was accepted for part-time studies at the Guildhall School of Music in London, where I studied opera and lieder, managing to get into the chorus at Sadler's Wells for a couple of operas. This didn't pay well, and, as I had a wife and family to support by this time, I branched out into various entrepreneurial ventures, though still performing as a 'semi-pro' in the world of music, my speciality being operetta.

But through all this, poetry and writing played a large part in my life, and still do, and I am grateful to my wife for allowing me the freedom to continue with this.

Preface

I have always had a feeling for poetry, the rhythms and the use of words. Even as a child, my mother's love of poetry led me to Gray's *Elegy*, one of the most beautiful poems, and works like Kipling's *If.* The deep, heartfelt expression in these and other poems made me want to try my hand at writing poetry, and I wrote my first poem whilst at primary school towards the end of the Second World War.

Further poems followed, including *Nighttime*, the last line of which the collection gets its title, some inspired by nature, some by music, for which I have always had a great love, and some by life in general.

Contents

Nighttime

The throb of mighty engines coming over waters still,
The crying of some night-bird out upon some lonely hill,
That wanders down to meet the sea where land and ocean meet,
These, and the lapping of the waves, are all I hear
Upon this, my lonely seat.

Upon my lonely seat I perch, dry aloft on friendly quay,
Eager for each night-borne sound to touch my ear so lovingly.
I sit here where the fishermen sat and wonder if I might
Be listening to the sounds they heard on some forgotten
Summer's night.

If you should wish to eavesdrop upon those bygone days,
Then sit here at the water's edge...
And listen to the waves.

Days

Warm days with a helping of Sun;
Hot days that make the sweat run.
Rainy days when the sun doesn't shine,
And days when I'm feeling I'm just glad it's fine.

Petals that fall like wedding confetti;
Robins hunt worms that look like spaghetti.
Now blossom has gone and fruits soon appear,
A sign that the Summer's fine days are near.

But surely the Spring, with its promising rush,
When hedgerows are filled with the blossom's first blush,
Fills the heart of each soul which has nought to give,
And make us feel lucky our short lives to live.

From the days that we number upon this sweet Earth,
From the days in the cot when our mother gave birth,
To the days when we creak to our seat on the porch,
To the day when we finally hand in our torch ...

Are so few when we number the days of the Sun,
That's been there forever, since there was just one.
So let us give thanks for the good things in life,
Our home and our children, our husband or wife.

Spring Greens

They start when Spring is in the air,
On days when cold and dark despair
Have vanished, and the warming sun
Gives the feeling that life's just begun.

Then, in the sunshine's warming rays,
Above the fields where sheep may graze,
Above the bluebell's damask blue,
They spread their width where songbirds flew.

And insects many, in the folds,
Can eat away, their colours bold,
Safe from the predators' hungry eyes
Who'd view them as a tasty prize.

And when the Summer's gone at last,
And blistering days are a thing soon past,
They show us colour's full array
That lasts through Autumn's golden days.

But when the Winter's icy storm
Brings snow and hail deep drifts to form,
Summer's green is past belief,
Each one falls – the gentle leaf.

The Gardener

She looked so neat and tidy in her over-sized green boots
And wanted so to help in every way.
The trouble was, the weeds she pulled, enthusiastically,
Were bedding plants I'd planted just that day!

I'd never tried to stop her, for she was so very keen,
And I know she really meant to be my aide.
But with help like this, my garden would never blaze with colour,
Except for the weeds she'd left there, I'm very much afraid.

So now I gently steer her out to the potting shed,
Where the worst she'll do is plant some rows of seeds.
And the garden's like a rainbow, from Spring right through the Summer,
And I can cultivate the beds of brightly coloured weeds!

It's not that she's forgetful, or doesn't really care,
For she loves the garden, just as much as me.
And it's not a lack of memory that makes her get it wrong,
She hasn't learned – you see, she's only just turned three!

Dogs

The hunting horn blows strident in the field,
The hounds, full flow, are eager in the chase.
Their quarry knows to nothing will they yield,
And runs with terror on his russet face.

Beyond the manse they chase him, far away,
And leave the Vicar's dogs a-baying loud.
They're Spaniels, and they'd love to romp and play,
And join the throng they see as a passing crowd.

The Vicar's wife has hidden from the sound
The passing hunt are making in the chase.
Her Pekingese and Shih Tzu round her bound;
They are not hunters and know their place.

They are for decoration, nothing more,
And give their owners comfort being there...
The wagging tail, the friendly, lifted paw,
The soulful eyes raised from their favourite chair.

But when we take their presence to account,
We feed them, groom them, clear their many hairs;
We own them, pay the bills that always seem to mount...
Are they our pets, or are we really theirs?

The Empty Window

The house that stands beneath the hill,
So empty and forlorn,
With windows that have lost their glass,
Beyond that ragged lawn.

Like empty eyes the windows gaze
Across the meadows green,
With memories they alone recall,
Of sights that they have seen.

It was a century ago,
The family were young,
The children played behind the glass,
And Christmas hymns were sung.

The men were called to battle,
The women wept in fear,
Their men were gone, might not return;
They shed a silent tear.

And so the mighty conflict took
The bravest from their home.
No more they'd reap their harvest;
No more their fields they'd roam.

The families left behind must move
And find another dwelling.
The house, now derelict, still stood,
A monument in its telling.

Though gales may tear at rustic eaves,
And storms its walls may soak,
It stands unmoved, through all these trials,
Like a great majestic oak.

And though the ghosts of bygone years,
Through the window frames may stare,
They cannot tell us what they saw;
Their knowledge they can't share.

For what they know is history,
It won't come round again,
Though we may stand and stare like them,
Through that broken windowpane.

Thoughts

What is a thought but a lightening bolt,
That suddenly springs from the gloom?
Like the brightest light that flashes out
In the dark, in an empty room.

What is a dream, but a hoped-for whim,
In the deepest sleep at night;
And nobody knows where they come from,
And why they vanish in light.

And what is hope, just something
That a yearning heart may desire,
That lies in the deepest, innermost breast,
Like a slowly smouldering fire.

So why, I ask, do I seldom dream?
Have I no wish to compete?
Perhaps I'm in luck with the life I've got
It's just that my life's been so sweet.

Fate's Dealings

I'm nearing the end of a fairly long life,
And I know that my luck has been great,
With my wife and my kids, and a clear, open mind,
I can leave all the rest to my Fate.

For Fate will deal cards that I cannot change
Or alter, if I had the chance.
But I must accept what the future may hold
And lead Fate the merriest dance!

Do I want to travel to far-distant shores?
Go exploring in jungles so deep?
Or visit the Outback, where no man has trod,
Where under the stars I may sleep?

But though I may wander, in years I have left,
And roam through countryside strange,
The places I visit may please me a lot
And allow me the freedom to range.

But when I have ranged through these strange, foreign climes,
And sated my lust for such travel,
I know I can come to my homeland again
And just let my spirit unravel.

For my home will still welcome me, tired and worn out,
As I sit in my chair by the fire
And relish the past I've been lucky to have,
Let my dreams all my children inspire.

The Dreamer

I could have done much better,
I could have been a star;
I could have been an astronaut,
Or driven a racing car.

I could have been ship's Captain,
And sailed the Seven Seas,
Or maybe been a clergyman
And spent life on my knees!

And what about a builder,
Who builds cathedrals tall?
Or an architect whose aspirations
Gives us shopping malls?

And don't forget the General,
Who through the ranks has risen;
Or the warder who has studied hard,
And runs the largest prison.

And then there are policemen,
And postmen by the score,
And the man who runs our Sainsbury's,
And many, many more.

You see I'm sliding down the scale,
Through all the great professions.
I'm coming down to earth just now,
With what are called confessions.

The truth, if I should tell it,
And what I want to be,
Comes down to this, my dearest friend,
I'm happy to be me.

Wishing

Where fleecy clouds caress the hills,
Where toucans clack their giant bills,
Where river rides provide such thrills
I wish I were there!

Where desert sand gets in your toes,
Where icebergs fill the icy floes,
Where the land is sterile and nothing grows
I wish I were there!

Where children never squawk and scream,
Where fish in thousands fill the stream,
Where snow provides the skiers dream,
I wish I were there!

Where giant trees stand tall, aloof,
Where igloos grant the only roof,
Where the only transport is on hoof,
I wish I were there!

But having traipsed the world around,
To places where there is no sound,
No loving family to be found
I wish I were home!

That Northern Land

The sunlight flickering on the quiet loch,
The heron gliding on the crystal air,
The seal's quiet flapping on the sun-dried rock,
The pine's still beauty on the mountain fair.

The grassy banks where youngsters play,
The trout streams shimmering in silver light,
The endless length of each summer's day,
That never wants to usher in the night.

The night that comes is brief as a Mayfly's life,
And nature stills the silence o'er the land.
The crofter lays a-weary by his wife
His work is solely by the strength of hand.

Though far from cities and their vibrant ways,
The northern islands lie amidst wild seas;
Their summers short, their winters have no days,
And yet their beauty can so many please.

This troubled world has many a country fair,
Though strife has put them far beyond our reach.
But Scotland stands untroubled and it's where
I shall return to find that lonely beach.

This land of kilt and sporran, grouse and deer,
Of Highland Games and many a golf course green,
Has magic, some may say, that has no peer
And sadly, little of it seen.

But now my travels take me far and wide,
To places where the thistle is not known.
Return I shall to sample Scotland's pride,
To burn and brae, where wildest winds have blown.

Spring

The starkness of the branches as I walk along the lane,
The freezing coldness of the showers of February rain;
The dormant bulbs that lie beneath the frozen, stubborn land,
Remind me that we're still not free from winter's icy hand.

Then March's blast of northern winds that crack and burn the face,
Are softened by the sudden warmth when flowers our gardens grace.
There are daffodils and hyacinths, and Scilla's haunting blue,
That make a swathe of colour and enhance the wintry view.

But April's gentle warmth pervades the gardens and the fields;
The countryside its beauty and its plenteous crops shall yield.
From planted seed to giant trees they all will gain their strength,
April's coloured days increase to give them summer's length.

So now we can look forward to the fullest blooms of May,
And endless sunshine as we near the perfect summer's day.
But even when we see it all, through crystal windowpane,
We know we'll soon be sheltering from that dread, incessant rain.

Seeds

The gale-force wind that blows strong,
The branches bend and cry.
The leaves and seeds blow merrily along,
Taken from their tree, away they fly.

Eventually, the seeds will come to rest
And settle in some secret crack or nook.
They germinate, some die, but still those left will do their best
To seek the sunlight, lift their face to look

Upon the world that waits for them to grow
Into majestic trees and saplings strong,
Though years may pass before we come to know
Their size – and then we do them wrong.

The woodsman and his axe will chop them down,
Away they go to factory or yard,
And there their fate is sealed, dependant on how they've grown,
And if their wood is decorative and hard.

For many trees their fate is commonplace,
The paper-mill awaits the tree's arrival.
They have no time, no given days of grace;
There is no question of their chance survival.

And into pulp for paper now they're ground,
For many's the need for paper in this world.
No substitute for paper's yet been found,
And when it's used, the paper then is hurled

Back to the wind that gave the seed its chance,
And floats across the parkland by me blown.
Full circle, as I watch the paper dance;
It rots away – and helps the seeds to grow.

The Shape of Days

Who gave the fields their pleasant shape,
Who filled them with the noisome rape,
That yellow shawls on hillsides drape?
The sturdy yeoman farmers.

In olden days it was their measure
That made the land our Nation's treasure;
Gave us all the time for leisure,
This wealth that is our land.

We taught the world the way to play,
The way to spend each leisured day,
And how to find the time to pray,
When working hours were done.

For work's for those who've not the time
To find the hours for nature's rhyme,
And do not need to seek the lime
Out in the public eye.

But with the way we've tamed the work,
We have no need the tasks to shirk,
Nor feel the Master's presence lurk
In hours we spend at play.

For hours at play help minds create,
And aid the quieter tongues to state
Their views, their thoughts, and pull their weight
Throughout a busy life.

So that, when all is said and done,
You've done your work and had your fun,
And you have all your distance run,
You've left a wealth behind.

For everyone leaves worthwhile days,
Though not, perhaps, in books or plays;
A little in the memory stays
To prove that once we lived.

Only the Wind

Only the wind knows where it's been,
Where it's travelled and what it's seen;
Laid its caress on damask cheek,
And travelled on to lands so bleak.

The soft and sultry breezes blow,
Round gentle hills in lands we know,
Down valleys soft as velvet's touch
Through flowery meadows filled with such

Pure gentle beauty that the breeze,
Gaining momentum from the sea's
Rough waves and tides and crashing foam,
Blows lightly inland to our home.

And there, our doors and windows flung
Wide open to see where flags are hung,
In village square, outside the church,
The breeze blows, as if in search.

And there it finds those flags to flap,
And makes those window-shutters clap
Like hands applauding brilliant deeds...
But only the wind can sow the seeds

Of monsoon, typhoon, blizzard, storm,
And many other frightful form
Of Mother Nature's awesome power
That causes timorous man to cower.

But onward blows that tireless air,
From zephyrs to storms beyond compare.
A breeze once started finds no rest,
No sleep at all in its endless quest.

Beaches

What is a beach but a golden strand
Of tiny pebbles, grains of sand,
That interferes and causes woes
In between those tiny toes.

But beaches are just Heaven sent
For children who, on play intent,
Will frolic till the day's long end
And then, must sadly, homeward wend

Their weary way with parents who,
Exhausted, must their duty do
And see their children off to bed,
So they can get their papers read.

But beaches right throughout the land
Can offer more than stones and sand,
And grant us all the chance to take
Their beauty for their beauty's sake.

For lonely beaches offer more
When viewed close to, along the shore,
Where sea-birds make their eerie cries,
Wheeling and swooping as waves rise

Before they touch that golden beach
Which human feet could never reach,
Because tall cliffs that beach surround,
And man, although this land has found,

Has never managed to explore
This dark, forbidding stretch of shore
That stood like this before man came
With cans and bottles, bringing shame

And spoiling all that nature made,
Without the use of fork or spade,
And spreading litter far and wide
Beyond the reach of the highest tide

That might this golden stretch then preen,
And leave it pure and shining clean,
As it was before man cursed this land,
And ruined every golden strand.

Diamonds from Dunghills

Do we stroll the countryside,
Or do we walk in towns?
Amble in the shopping malls,
Or stride the Sussex Downs?

Watch the men in fishing boats,
Working at their nets,
Or spend our time in villages,
The ones that Time forgets?

Sadly, many never see
The countryside in bloom;
They spend their active waking hours
In many a stifling room.

They earn their monstrous wages,
Seated at computer screens,
With never a thought of what might lie
Behind those rustic scenes.

They sneer, they scoff at rural folk,
They never have the time
To visit, to explore their worth,
To know their rural rhyme.

For many-a-folk who dwell these days
Beyond the city's line,
Are worth a thousand, thousand fold
Of a city-dweller's kind.

For jewels they be, these country folk,
Though they by the midden dwell;
They scorn the concrete jungle,
And think of it as Hell.

Dreaming

Lazy days, skies full of blue,
Fields of grass of a verdant hue.
Skylarks singing overhead,
Till the evening sky turns a fiery red.

Peaceful days, with little care,
Bees hum in the silken air.
Woodpeckers knock on the broken tree;
Scones and jam are laid for tea.

Careless days with little to worry,
Magpies hunt for defenceless quarry.
Cuckoos sound in the woodland near,
Hunting for nests their eggs to bear.

Wonderful days, when all seems right,
From opening dawn to closing night.
Flowers full of scent that fills the air,
Teasing the nostrils of all who care.

Busy days, when work must be done;
Days when you'd rather be having fun,
Instead of sitting at your desk all day,
You'd rather be dreaming in a field of hay.

Nature

I'm lying in the sunshine by a field of golden corn,
With a skylark busy singing overhead.
He sings his song so beautifully, and soars his easy flight,
Till the evening sky is turning fiery red.

The evening clouds are gathering to mark the end of day;
I hear an owl that hoots in a nearby field.
A fox is barking as it hunts to feed its hungry cubs,
And rabbits to the weasel's stare will yield.

The hunting and the hunted fill the evening air with sound,
Though to many the interpretation's lost,
For those who live within the walls of busy towns and cities,
Seldom see the countryside, in sunshine or in frost.

And though I now must live my life in easy reach of all,
The countryside will always draw me back,
To the lovely sound of silence – or something close to nature –
To see the night-time sky that's almost black.

The skylark now no longer sings but crouches in its nest,
And starlight gives the land a ghost-like gleam.
So I shall still return here, and let my memory roam,
As I take my seat beside a woodland stream.

The Last Dodo

Imagine you're that Dodo,
With nothing much to do,
But search around the island
For someone just like you.

And therein lies the problem,
Which never seems quite fair,
For search and search as best you may,
There's simply no one there.

Trapped!

I'm trapped inside my tiny mind,
And I long to set me free!
But how can I hope to do this,
When all I am is me?

I'm trapped in a gentle marriage,
With lots of love and care;
But perhaps the me that wants to be free
Just longs for the open air!

I'm trapped in a pulsing motor car,
In a mile-long traffic jam,
And I curse and swear at the cars around,
Because I'm where I am.

I'm trapped in a house on a vast estate,
With folk I can never know,
'Cos all I see through my windowpane
Is the folk that just come and go.

I'm trapped in a train on my way to work,
Because there are leaves on the line,
And the queue to the loo is a very long queue;
I mustn't have so much wine!

I'm trapped in an office at journey's end,
And there I must spend my days,
'Cos the job I've got, though I sweat a lot,
Is the only job that pays.

I'm trapped in a family roundabout,
And my family come and go.
I love them all, both young and old,
'Cos they're all I've got to show.

I'm trapped in my body until I die,
There's no alternative.
So I'll try to be happy, and love and laugh,
As long as I may live.

The Lost World

When humans may no longer be
The ruling class on earth,
And even those remaining
Cannot recollect their birth,
Machines may be our masters,
A very serious thought,
For we, the fragile human,
Their given knowledge taught.

And as we humans fade away,
Our numbers even less,
Machines will rule our futures,
For we've made a total mess
Of everything we've ever learned
And have ourselves to blame;
We cannot curse the 'monsters',
If we have to give a name

To the awkward, angled, clanking things
That stride the empty streets,
As we no longer use our brains
And even less our feet!
And what of all the famous works
Of man's creative mind?
Machines won't give a tuppeny cuss
For what we've left behind!

Shakespeare's greatest writings,
Schubert's beautiful songs;
Many other wondrous works
For which the heart still longs.

A million years will pass away,
Will anyone recall
The greatest works of art that passed
Along through memory's hall?

It makes me sad to ponder.
Among the monster's dross,
That all of man's creative art
Has totally been lost.

So why do we all bother?
Why do we all strain?
When reckoning for the future,
They'll never see our like again.

The River Bank

I sit here on the river bank,
And watch the water flow.
I don't know where it's come from,
And I don't know where it'll go.

It sweeps past so majestically,
When it is in full spate.
How fish can stay within its bounds
It's hard to contemplate.

But live they do, within its depths,
And eat and mate and breed,
Hiding from their predators
In many a-close grown reed.

Whether Pike or Perch or stickleback,
They each may have their place,
And fill the glorious streams we have
With their swarming, finny race.

And now I watch the Kingfisher,
How aptly named is he,
Diving from a lofty branch
A flash that few may see.

And Otters, Mink and Water Shrews,
Herons, Moorhens and Coots,
Will occupy my questing gaze
Among the treeless roots.

And so I sit in peaceful calm,
With the whispering stream at my feet.
Happy to be at one with my soul
And what nature I may meet.

Wildwood

I stood in the deep of the valley,
Not a sound in the woodland heard,
Though I strained my ears for something,
Be it man, or beast, or bird.

The trees climbed high around me,
Their arms stretched to the sky,
And I stared at the trees and I wondered,
If there was a reason why?

For the trees are so much taller,
And their roots go burrowing deep,
And with all that pulsing life within
Is it possible that they sleep?

But the answer came from the breeze above,
And their branches waved to the sky,
And the birds flew off in wild alarm,
And I now knew the reason why.

The trees and the valley have long been here,
Before man came along,
And years after we have shed this coil,
The trees will still sing their song.

For their song is the song of the Wildwood,
I felt it standing there,
As a puny, insignificant man,
I felt it throb in the air.

And beauty remains in the Wildwood,
In the forests and clearings wide,
For the trees are there for all to see
They've nothing at all to hide.

But I knew I never could sing their song,
They were words that I'd never know.
For their secret still lies in the Wildwood,
In places we cannot go.

Should We Care?

When all the music's over,
When all the books are read;
When the writing's all been written,
And the words have all been said.

When the birds have stopped their singing,
And the sun has ceased to shine;
When all the food's been eaten,
And we've drunk the last of the wine.

When all the seas are drying,
And all the trees are bare,
And everyone is homeless,
And no one seems to care.

When the land is now infertile,
And the seeds just will not grow,
And there isn't any petrol,
And there's nowhere left to go.

The fish have all been poisoned
And the animals are dead;
We cannot grow the wheat we need
For making loaves of bread.

Perhaps we will then realise
Each day cannot be sunny,
And everyone will come to learn
You can't just live on money.

Flower

Pause when you see a tiny flower,
The present hour may be its last.
For tiny flowers will come and go,
Without the chance for us to know
The beauty that has passed.

Such transient beauty should not fade,
But nature takes its toll,
And all returns from whence it came,
Even man with all his claims to fame,
Is naught but nature's moll.

For though we strive to live our lives,
And seek eternal bliss,
Our chance of immortality,
Escaping death's reality,
Amounts to less than this.

For though we think we've climbed the hill
And are riding on the wave
That sweeps man on at centuries' call
Remember now that blossom small
That triumphs on our grave.

For peerless beauty has that flower,
And sculptured is its grace,
And though man learns a thousand things,
And reaches stars on mighty wings,
The blossom wins the race.

For when our day has been and gone,
And all we've left is dust,
The flowers will still be blooming free,
Untrammelled by man's history;
The world is in their trust.

Grasslands

The years have come and gone, my friends,
I hardly saw them pass.
Now other generations fill
Those places on the grass.

Where once I romped and played the games
The other children played,
And sought my ball that found its way
To where the lovers laid.

They never moved, they did not hear,
They couldn't feel, they couldn't see;
Their love controlled their every sense,
So much they never noticed me.

The fond embrace was all they wanted,
Minds lost in a trance.
They never saw the youthful feet
That dashed and darted in the dance.

For dance we did in those fields of grass,
Till the shadows sent us flying,
Our energy full spent at last,
It embers glowing, dying.

But now those lover's time is over,
They have moved to a higher sphere.
I am now the Oldest Member,
Now I'm in my eightieth year.

Life has now a pace more gentle,
Limbs once supple bend no more,
I can hardly make the distance
To the grasslands from my door.

Perhaps I shouldn't really bother,
Make my own contentment here,
Leaving wandering to the others…
Others that I hold so dear.

It's my children's children's turn,
Playing by the stream;
I shall watch them from a distance,
Warming in my dream.

But my eyes no longer see
What there is before me;
Only what my heart remembers,
What I *want* there still to be.

Fall

The weeks and months go by at Season's call;
The Summer's ended, now we face the Fall,
When grasses fade with heat, and leaves turn brown,
And fruits of orchard ripen and fall down.

Beneath the trees that lately blossomed well,
Where pears and apples, plums and damsons fell,
The farmer's wife allows her flock to graze,
To eat their fill, to combat Winter's days.

Along the hedgerow now the silence holds,
As Autumn takes its grip along the folds,
And later, icy fingers of the Winter's frost,
Persuade the farmer now to count the cost.

For Autumn is the harvest's latest time;
All should be gathered e'er the frosty rime
Kills all the crops not gathered on the farm,
For Autumn leads to Winter, and great harm

To crops not gathered, stacked and stored,
And grain into the giant silo poured.
But Autumn in itself creates a glory,
A beauty in a hedge, a tree, a story

That is told in colours of a russet hue,
That always lends enchantment to the view;
To make a painter's palette for our eyes,
Which slowly dies beneath the Autumn skies.

For now the latest Summer's passed along,
No more the hedgerows ring with songbird's song,
But stillness creeps into the dying land.
We know, ere long, we'll feel the frosty hand

Of Winter, as it steals its way around
Each copse, each wood, towards our homestead bound.
But we'll offer thanks at our Harvest Festival,
For what has been Autumn's Carnival.

Autumn 1

The leaves of Autumn fall like bright confetti for the bride;
The trees are looking naked down the shady woodland ride;
The birds are falling silent in the stillness of the day,
As Autumn gently eases in, waves Summer on its way.

The final leaves are hanging on the bones of every tree,
Like skeletons they're standing, from their raiment they are free.
The hedgerows now prepare themselves for Winter's icy blast
The only consolation, as we know, it cannot last.

For Spring will come and Summer's glorious days,
The days when meadows shimmer in the misty, heat-filled haze.
E'er long the Summer's days are gone, too fast, at Autumn's call,
As here we are, once more, at the season's fall.

Alternative Leisure
(With apologies!)

What is this life, if full of care,
We have no time to stand and stare.

No time to stand when shops we pass,
And press our noses to the glass.

No time to find a simple pound
For those whose home is on the ground.

No time to spend an hour or four,
Sipping wine – and ask for more.

No time to spend on a Summer's day,
Rolling around in a field of hay.

No time, engrossed in a busy life,
To spend some time with one's lovely wife.

No time to watch life's merry-go-round,
Before we are laid in the ground.

No time to wonder where life's gone,
And remember how the sun has shone.

No time to see, not mow the grass,
And wonder where the days have passed.

No time to wander in a woodland glade,
Or sip a drink in the welcome shade.

No time to lean on a farmyard gate,
Or see a river in full spate.

Just time to rush and dash about,
And hear the neighbour's noisy shout.

A poor life this, if full of care,
We have no time to stand and stare.

Why?

I lay on my back in my garden
And stared at the starry sky.
I found that I was wondering,
If there was a reason why?

What held the stars in the firmament,
And gave them the strength to remain,
So high and fixed in their orbits,
And stopped them falling like rain.

And the Moon, like some heavenly beauty,
Graces the skies above,
As an aid to those young couples courting,
And the poets searching for love.

But is it not faintly conceivable
That there's life in those far-distant blips?
Or are they just holes in the firmament,
Which let in those rain-bearing drips?

I like to think that it's possible,
As I lay and stared at the sky,
That there's folk up there in the Universe –
And that *they* may be wondering why.

Imprisoned

I like to see the countryside,
Both nearby and afar;
But why do I only see it
Through the windows of my car?

For like so many others
Who have so little time,
I drive around until I've found
A scene that's free from grime.

The hillsides and the pastures,
The woodland and the stream,
Make many bucolic pictures
In a cinematic dream.

I promise I'll go walking,
Perhaps through a shady glade,
Hoping I perchance will meet
Some pretty, winsome maid!

But I seldom seem to leave it,
My noisy, smelly car,
Unless I find a place to eat,
Or a smoke-filled, young folks bar.

Perhaps one day I'll take a chance
And open wide my door,
And run along the bush-banked lanes,
Or across the woodland floor.

And see the things I used to see
So many years ago;
Remembering where I caught the fish,
Against the river's flow.

But scenes like these have gone now,
From everybody's view;
It's easier to use the car
And do what others do.

We drive to here, we drive to there,
In lines of cars we drive;
Always, always travelling…
But we never do arrive.

Autumn 2

Autumn is upon us and the fields are turning brown;
The farmer's done his duty, and the crops have been cut down.
Out there in the stack-yard, the sheaves are climbing high,
In children's eyes it seems they will one day reach the sky.

The Autumn fruits hang heavy in the hedge along the lane.
I wonder, shall I live to see another Fall again?
For Time is passing, like a tide, that never can turn back,
And now I see that russet sky is turning a frightening black.

The heavy clouds that gather as the storm sweeps on its way,
Make the farmer glad it's not the time to harvest fields of hay.
The geese fly low across his fields, chattering as they pass;
He hopes it's not his fields they'll find, and crop like fields of grass.

The Redwings and the Lapwings next appear in swarming flight,
Though seldom in the Summer will you see the glorious sight
They make as through the sky they pass, on mysterious journies bound,
When suddenly they fall like leaves in Autumn to the ground.

The estuary is crowded now with Winter's migrants flight,
Some going south, some north, through Autumn's flickering light.
How can they find their way back here, and land with a thousand feet,
When I can't find my way back home, wandering down the street?

November is the Autumn's end, before the Winter's start,
And all is still within the woods, the Ring Dove's call apart.
For creatures start to hibernate, before the snow's first fall;
Like the countryside, they'll sleep till they hear the Spring's first call.

But that's a long way off, my friends, and first we have to face
A Winter's snows, until they thaw, and make some streams to race
Across the meadows, through the woods, and down to the mighty sea,
That's unaffected by the seasons, unlike you and me.

But we're still here, and face the Fall with a humble heart,
For there's nothing we can do to help to hasten Summer's start.
So let's enjoy the beauty that we find along the lane,
And hope and pray that we shall grasp the Season's joy again.

Autumn's Coming

The Summer now is over, and the fields are turning brown;
The Farmer's done his duty – the crops have been cut down.
Bales of straw lay scattered as the combine passes by
And there they'll stay till on the haywain they are piled so high.

The hedgerow's lost its glamour now the boughs are looking bare;
The leaves are brown and shrivelled in the colder Autumn air.
The nests that once were occupied are empty and forlorn,
And songbirds now can spend their time heralding the dawn.

But Autumn has its pleasures in stillness that's serene;
A freshness that pervades the air, and keeps the landscapes clean.
The branches bare are washed afresh by early morning rain,
In readiness for snow's bright mantle, sparkling clean again.

The woods where Fox and Badger hunt their most elusive prey,
Are still and silent with their absence with the coming of the day.
For all must know that Winter's coming isn't far ahead,
When all those that hibernate seek their dark and private bed.

But seasons in their ripeness, like the fruit upon the tree,
Must reach their own conclusions, for each of us to see.
And though the Winter's coming and fills us all with dread,
We can follow Fox and Badger … and take ourselves to bed!

The Infinity

I lay on my back in my garden,
And gazed up into space.
Was I looking for depth in the Universe,
Or trying to see the Moon's face.

A million stars were shining,
With a billion planets around.
Was there life in these far distant objects,
For I heard not a single sound.

Except, that is, for the breezes
That soughed through the nearby trees,
But these never reached to the heavens,
Though they ruffled the oceans and seas.

But shooting stars were a-plenty,
Though possibly they were man-made,
And sent up to give us the answers
To the questions that science essayed.

But if they were man-made objects,
Stars we'd put in the sky,
Did they ever answer the questions,
And tell us the reasons why.

The stars could hang in the canopy,
Arcing right over our head.
When, given the forces of gravity,
They might fall to the ground instead.

The Future?

Let's go back a hundred years,
Before computers came,
When conversation was an art,
And lovers played the game.

Before the days of radio,
When all we had to watch
Were bubbles rising in a glass,
Or the measure of the Scotch.

Three hundred years before that time,
King Henry's day was done,
And all the locals had to do
Was sit round in the sun.

But little chance the poor folk had,
For theirs was a hard-lived life,
And everyone then worked the land,
The husband, child and wife.

Ten thousand years before we came
To grace this noble land,
They dwelt in caves, hard by the sea,
And lived by strength of hand.

Think back a hundred million years,
The dinosaurs were waning;
And mammals fought to make their stand,
Every sinew straining.

Four billion years ago, we're told,
This globe was a ball of gas,
That cooled and then solidified,
And our future came to pass.

But now we've reached a turning point,
Our world's in a total mess.
Will we return to a ball of gas
Or maybe something less?

Roads

I've travelled many lonely roads
In searching for my goal,
But still have reached no journey's end
In questing for my soul.

From Kansas' prairie grasslands wide,
To Oz's golden sands,
Each has a beauty unexplained,
Like the road to Samarkand.

This road was known a thousand years
Before I walked this earth,
So why should I feel somehow drawn
Around this planet's girth?

For distant places have a charm
That pulls me from my chair,
To travel on in hopeless hope
And end in deep despair.

For though each time I sally forth
To seek some Holy Grail,
And visit busy, bustling towns,
I end down some lonely trail.

Perhaps the loneliness I find
Is what I really seek,
And I do not need that hard impact
From living cheek by cheek.

For the closeness of humanity
Of every race and creed,
Though worthy men they all may be,
Is something I don't need.

And though I love my fellow man,
And my family is most dear,
It's solitude that does the most
To make thoughts crystal clear.

So that lonely isle, that lonely tree,
Mean more to me each year,
In the timeless, changeless way they have,
Than all you hold most dear.

But loneliness of heart is something
That I'll never find,
For the love you've always given me
Will ever be on my mind.

Autumnal Scene

The Autumn scents caress the gently wandering breeze,
And songbirds once so vocal now are still.
The beaches empty by the silent sea,
And tractors purr away on distant hill.

The combines leave the fields like well-combed hair,
And hedgerows lose their fullness and their flower.
The countryside is left to the farmer's care,
The woodland now becomes a secret bower.

Full-throated though the songbirds were at dawn,
When Summer sun had risen o'er the field,
Their silence now a heaviness had drawn,
As if no sound their little lungs could yield.

The butterflies and bees that found the flowers
So nectar-laden for their daily feast,
Have hibernated and their body cowers,
Deep-hidden against Winter's icy beast.

For nothing save the Spring's forthcoming warm
Can rouse their tiny bodies from their sleep,
And bring them forth the countryside to swarm,
And form our childhood's memories so deep.

For now though, as the Winter comes,
And stillness closes down the land at last,
All creatures great and small hide in their homes.
Autumn's gone; they shelter from the blast

That sweeps the land and cleans the harvest scene,
And lays the breast of nature open wide.
When Spring arrives, with Beauty dressed in green,
All memories of Winter we can hide.

The Evening

Dawn is a very special time,
When the mists lie over the land,
And the view across the wooded vale
Is shaped by a spectral hand.

But ghostly work, as the sun comes up,
Fades quickly from the sight,
And the mists among the silent trees
Give way to the morning light.

And as the day's bright morning rays
Thread through the sylvan glades,
The memories of the previous night
Are lost in the wakening shades.

And heaven's bright orb that is the Sun,
Climbs into a brazen sky
And who remembers the starry vault
Or even questions why?

When mists arise in the evening's calm
And smother the trees and the land,
The softest breeze among those trees,
Has the sound of a ghostly band.

But for those who venture forth at night,
Among the trees in the lane,
Their reward is the peace and quiet they find
And may never find again.

Nature Watch

Time passes like a flowing stream,
The poets used to say,
And now I'm getting older,
Each day just flies away.
The days I used to treasure,
In ice or snow or sun,
Seem distant when I view them,
But I loved them, every one.

That fleeting flight of butterflies,
That swarm of honey bees,
Would send me hunting for their homes,
In places no one sees.
The secrets of the wildlife
Then held me in their thrall,
And in the long grass I would lie,
To witness nature's call.

It seemed I was impervious
To nature's cruellest sting.
I lay there in the sunshine,
And how my heart did sing!
For days I would collect them,
And set their tiny wings,
But now I find I wonder,
What made me do such things.

For every tiny mite I took,
And pinned it to my boards,
Was a crime against our nature –
What made us think we're Lords?
But now I watch the empty skies,
And long for their return,
When springtime warms the grasslands,
And the sun begins to burn.

But watch I may, for days in vain,
And little do I see.
We stole those tiny creatures
From the World's posterity.
Our children now are suffering,
For the countryside is 'clean.'
We've sprayed and killed all living things
Now they watch a computer screen.

Time

Although I've little else to do
But sit here, thinking thoughts of you,
I do not feel my life is wasted,
For so many joys I've tasted.

Centuries ago it seems
I dreamed the dreams that all men dream.
I'd conquer worlds both far and near,
And find those things all men hold dear.

But travel, broadening the mind,
Cannot replace what's left behind.
The loved ones gone from nature's plain
That we shall never see again.

Perhaps that's why I roam no more,
But sit here, quietly, by my door;
Content for all the world to know
There's nowhere else I want to go.

And here I'll stay till my day is done,
My life well lived, my race well run.
My love I'll give to one and all,
Till I travel again at that last great call.

Snowfall

The snow that falls and covers every lawn,
And fills the tiny crevices at dawn;
The freezing hand that grips the palm of man
When first he wakes and thence does scan
A whitened view, that only yesterday
Was green and pleasant with the smell of hay.

The frost that lives with snow when it does fall,
And rimes the trees and bushes, short and tall,
To trace their lacy elegance in white,
Like spectral figures in the icy night,
And makes each span of water into glass…
A mirror for each face as it may pass.

For children, such a time for play is meant,
For ice and snow have purpose, heaven sent.
Their bones are young, and falls they take with grace,
Although a tear may streak their frozen face.
They build their snowmen – inch by inch they climb –
Until at last they're told 'It's supper time!'

But for the old a different story waits,
For icy patches doom their stiffened gaits.
Each step is taken with the utmost care,
And children's games are more than they would dare.
Too soon the frozen depths of death's cold state
Await them all – no man can contemplate

The eternity of cold that is man's lot.
So, while he may, he'll savour somewhere hot,
And leave the ice and snow to those so young,
For whom a fall of snow is an anthem sung,
And sit and watch the generations pass
He sees himself when young, as in a timeless, frozen glass.

The Graveyard

I wandered through the graveyard in the stillness of the dawn,
With a hundred mossy headstones looking on...
And wondered, in the stillness, of the stories they might tell,
Of victories these folk had lost or won.

For victories are not for just the mighty and the rich,
'Cos ordinary folk can be as brave,
Though the triumphs that they muster may never, never reach
The ears and eyes of those who view the grave.

But gravestones only tell us the barest bones of life,
The dates we came and left this wondrous Earth;
And nothing on our gravestones can tell those watching eyes
Of man or woman's triumphs or their worth.

Yet every man and woman has a story they can tell,
Although it may not ever grip the heart.
For life itself's a story, from the cradle to the grave,
And every man and woman plays a part.

But those gravestones that we see, as we wander by the church,
Are cold and enigmatic, every one,
For all their surface tells us is a listing of the dead,
And nothing of life's sadnesses and fun.

Two hundred years ago, when these folk were laid to rest,
All their worldly goods their tribute paid.
They left this world with everything they'd brought in at their birth;
Their family a tiny posy laid.

It laid upon their coffin, and those who stood and mourned
Were the only ones who gave their story life;
For when the folk who knew them have also passed away,
Their story passed away as well, their triumphs, loves and strife.

November

The leaves fall in gale-blown drifts;
A gloom descends upon the land.
Autumn's lustre now has flown,
Before November's wintry hand.

The earlier shine that filled the trees
With blossom and a Springtime gift,
Is now forgotten, Winter's near,
The time approaches for the snowy drift.

But long before the snow quick falls
That cloaks the land with an icy grip;
The ditches filled by heavy rain,
And raindrops down the window drip.

They make lined patterns down the pane,
Through Summer's dust that still is there;
Mazy tracings that a child,
Kneeling, watches from a chair.

They love the warmth from the blazing fire,
The comfort of surrounding walls;
The knowledge that they're safe inside,
Before November palls.

But though we dread November's worst,
And cling together through the storm,
With Christmas just a month away,
Remember, this is just the norm.

And when November's over,
And the New Year's close at hand,
Forget the worst that Winter brings
Spring will soon embrace the land.

The Winter Snow

Goodbye dread snow, I want no more
There, deep-drifting by my door.
Bring forth the glorious warmth that tells
Of sunlight's bright uplifting spells.

My garden's cloaked in Winter's sheen,
The ice that dulls the lawn's bright green,
Where bulbs lie dormant, sleeping there,
Waiting for the Spring's warm air

To thrill them with the faintest brush
That heralds first that blooming rush
That shows when through the soil they burst,
All-rushing, perhaps, to be the first

To bless the view the garden shows
Where every sunlit flower soon grows.
For now, though, we must be content –
Just feel that eagerness, well meant.

For hail and snow, that Winter wind that hones
Our footpath's ice that may break our bones,
Will pass, and in a month or two,
Warm sunshine gladdens every view.

Does Anyone Care?

What are we but dust-motes,
In the way the poet's rhyme?
Each tiny effort we may make
In the greatest stretch of time,
Is nothing but the merest tick
In Time's great turning wheel,
And nothing we can make or do
Can make a human feel
That they can change the Universe,
Or bring the Moon to Earth,
Or make it spin the other way…
That way we'd know our worth.

Only a tiny man you are,
In a tiny city dwell;
In a tiny house, in a tiny town,
Trapped in a tiny hell.
And no one who lives beyond the Moon,
If there's anyone out there,
Could possibly know, or want to learn,
What makes our lives so fair.

Only a tiny man you are,
You and your tiny wife;
In a tiny house, in a tiny town,
Living your tiny life.
And no one who dwells, if dwell they do,
In lands beyond our ken,
Will turn a hair, or trouble to stare,
If your miniature Earth so full of care
Turns into a flaming sun.

The Haven

The sanctuary for a man
When sheltering from the rain,
Lies at the end of the garden,
Where he might muse again.

No traffic noise, no barking dogs,
Can reach his sheltered ears.
No screaming kids, no pleading wife,
Disrupt the peace of years.

This is his holy haven,
From which his thoughts might roam.
And others share this tranquil spot,
Make it their Winter home.

A tortoiseshell suspended there
Behind the curtain rail;
A Hedgehog cunningly concealed
Beneath an upturned pail.

A spider seeking comfort,
Spins her web to catch her prey,
Though little will fall victim
On this cold and frosty day.

But though there's little to be seen,
For sensible things have fled,
A man can always shelter
In his rustic garden shed.

The Window

Happy days I've spent beside the window of my house,
That looks across the fields towards the wood.
Although I cannot move from here, I cannot find the strength,
I know that's where I'd wander, if I could.

That distant wood, the sighing breeze, the carolling of birds,
Remind me of much younger days, when I was fit and strong,
When through the wooded glades I'd stroll, happy to be one
With nature in its glory, and that carried me along.

Folk asked if I was lonely in my isolated walks;
Did I not miss the company of friends?
But loneliness is something that the inner soul can quench,
And now this view I have can make amends.

My friends have sadly passed along, through Time's immortal lane,
So I shall sit and ponder in my quest,
And know the view I have now, through my lonely windowpane,
Is all I have, till I am – too – laid to rest.

That Vanished World

Many, many years ago, when I was very young,
Every day was sunny, every song was sung
By birds up in the tree-tops, which always seemed so green
And fields and streets and houses, always seemed so clean.

And people seemed so friendly when we played out in the street,
And an old man offered toffees to the children he would greet.
His smile was warm and genuine, he was always pleased to see
The youngsters at their hard-fought games, running fancy free,

For nothing seemed to blight their days, nothing made them care,
Nothing took away their fun, nothing stopped the dare
They made to other kids around to climb the graveyard wall,
Or steal the Vicar's apples from his trees so soaring tall.

Days so full of freedom, days so full of fun,
Days full of discovery for lives that have begun
To show how individuals their separate lives can trace,
And so befit them for their chance to grace the human race.

Those balmy days, so far away, when the world was a happy town,
And no one seemed to threaten us, or governments bring down.
Through children's eyes, so innocent, untouched by worldly cares
The worst thing that could happen was the other children's dares!

But times do change, as change they must, and everyone grows old,
And the happiness we knew as kids has suddenly grown cold.
For the world we knew and loved and shared with others of our kind,
Has gone, and all that's left is chaos, with the blind led by the blind!

Time's Running Out!

When there isn't any silver,
And there isn't any gold,
And we've used up all the minerals,
And the world is growing cold.

When the stars are all receding,
And the Moon has lost its glow;
The Sun is still expanding,
And the tides much swollen flow.

Now man must search among the stars
To find a place to dwell.
Be it on some lovely planet
Or a place that's more like Hell!

Our spaceships roam the Galaxy,
Searching for a home.
Their quest is seeming endless
They don't know where to roam.

Undoubtedly there are planets
Revolving out in space.
We know there are because we've seen them
As they cross a star's face

In distant lonely Galaxies,
Light years from our Sun,
Though the search we make to find them
Has only just begun.

But search we must, for time is short,
We haven't long to go,
Before our planet is consumed
By the solar inferno.

When I say 'we haven't long,'
What I really mean to say,
Is that we've only a billion years
Left for man to play!

Space

I lie on my back in my garden,
And stare at the Moon's gibbous face.
And beyond, in the darkening eternity,
Of the endless, boundless space.

Is it possible that there are peoples
On planets around distant suns?
Are there folk with long-distance telescopes?
Can we be the only ones

Who stare and stare into hyperspace,
Hoping and praying we'll find,
That others in far-distant places,
May be something like human-kind.

But if they've all got three heads and four legs,
And are lovely in each other's eyes,
How can we, in our far-distant world,
Stand here and then criticise?

For beauty's in the beholder's eyes,
Not written in orderly prose,
And the fact that those far-distant beings
Just don't have an ear or a nose,

Has nothing to do with the way they behave,
Or the beauty that other folk see,
But the spirit that lies within their souls,
Which is much more important to me.

Memory

Now I am old, and the future has no worth,
My mind will sometimes wander back towards my birth.
I'll see forgotten folk, who were my kin,
As gentlemen and ladies, free from sin.

Their passions and their wrath, their pomp and pride,
Were just like yours and mine, and hard to hide.
But time from future generations keeps
Their secrets, as in some vast and oceanic deep.

They had their loves, and wooed with ardent lust,
And went to war as ordered, as they must;
And some did die, before their passions filled,
And in their dying, saw their future killed.

But some remained, and those the young recall,
Though memory still plays tricks – they weren't *that* tall! –
But normal folk, who led such different lives,
For now there are few husbands and few wives.

For marriage in those days was meant to last,
And parting brought much sorrow to the cast
Who played the 'family game' as on a stage
But weddings now seem from a bygone age.

Perhaps we all must strive and do our best to make
A happy world, if only for the children's sake.
For they are blameless, and surely should not be
Cursed with the problems of the past, of history.

The Gravestones

How sad I see the churchyard as I walk along the lane.
I know I'll never have the chance to see those folk again.
Their lives are a distant memory, and all that's left is a stone,
That gives their dates of birth and death – we know their spirit's flown.

And all who stand and see the stone, and read their epitaph,
Can never know the highs and lows that made their lives a graph.
As a small child, so innocent, they played their little game,
And trouble, though it courted them, was always put to shame.

Their innocence did triumph, as they spent their youthful days,
In games around the Village Green, and in their simple ways,
They taught each other pleasures, and kept their spirits free
To venture forth into the world, and leave their mother's knee.

Their swords they drew in our defence, to keep our country safe.
They kept the enemy without, and every little waif
Who'd played around the Village Green, now grown into a man,
Would flex his little muscles, as only soldiers can.

When they returned from battle, with the victory they had won,
Their lives they then took up again, their fighting days were done.
They married, reared their children, led their lives in simple bliss,
But even then they dared to share a hidden, loving kiss.

For romance, for these couples, was a quiet, forbidden stance,
And even though they'd married, their love was a secret dance.
They stayed together, come what may, and loved to the end of time,
Though seldom would they dare to put their feelings in a rhyme.

The only rhyme was one that they could simply never know.
'Twas on their stone, in the churchyard, where the lofty weeds now grow.
But there it is, for all to see, a simple, moving verse,
That tells us naught about the folk now caught by death's cold curse.

Winter

How sad I feel when Winter's here,
With the passing of each Summer's day,
So full of promise, warmth and beauty.
Still, I shall not shed a tear,
No matter how deep the snow may lay.
To me each season does its duty.

Spring, the optimistic time;
Summer full of flowering gladness,
Autumn, tints of russet hues;
Winter, with frost's heavy rime,
And the dead leaves flying sadness
Under skies of icy blues.

Now the farmland's deepening brown,
And the hedge its berries shows;
Trees tall, leafless skeletons stand,
Their leaves long showered down.
The lonely bull by the field gate lows,
And the stillness is gripped by Winter's hand.

I dare not wander down the lane,
To where the 'Pig and Whistle' stands;
I dare not risk the snow and ice
I see through my frosty windowpane.
For Winter brings on aching glands,
And I dare not chance that snowy vice.

But sitting in my warm seclusion,
Rug wrapped round my aching knees,
Snug, away from frost's cold bite,
Cradling cups of tea's infusion,
Nibbling, drinking as I please,
I could stay here through the night.

And, suppose I took the chance
Of staying here, beside the fire,
Listening to the winter storm,
Will I again in the ballroom dance,
Or sing to the celestial lyre,
Or will I be found, a silent form?

It's all too easy, now I'm old,
And creak in every fragile bone,
To surrender the pleasures of the world,
So I'll sit here, safe from wet and cold.
I'll watch the world, its ever-changing tone,
And see the season's flags unfurled.

The Empty House

Oh empty house with wind-flapped shutters,
Missing tiles and leaf-filled gutters,
Many years have passed along
Since children ran with laugh and song
Through corridors and rooms whose walls
Echoed with their parents' calls.
Each room a dusty history holds,
From creaking boards to curtain folds,
And if those rooms a tale could say,
What wondrous moments they might lay
Upon the troubled, trembling earth
For everyone to judge their worth.
Tales of valour, romance, history,
Happy years, some full of mystery.
Yet the watcher of tomorrow
Cannot hope to catch the sorrow
That those human hearts did hold
But never could the world be told.
Tragedy and deepest grief,
Passion trapped beyond belief,
Suffocated in the breast,
Like a dagger in the chest.
Unrequited love that clung
Like a monstrous weight that hung,
Dragging downwards, ever down,
In deepest chasms there to drown.
Human hope and passion, love,
Precious gifts from Him above –
Every room must have its score,
Every corner there's a store
Of vibrancy in the dank, cold air,
And not just love, but dark despair;
The empty bed, the open door,
Tell tales of those who trod this floor;
Who'd filled the house with thoughts again
Ere emptiness began its reign.
And then, outside, that weedy patch,

The mossy roof, that thinning thatch,
Are evidence, for all who care
Just like the carpet on the stair
That's left in place, but badly worn,
Like wallpaper that's old and torn
They see a remnant of the past.
But just how long these things will last
Is open to the visitor's guess,
As everything's a holy mess
And though things stand in timeless stance,
Each day that comes must take its chance
To see the walls and chimney fall
As weeds and grime will cover all.
But hours and minutes, days and years,
Grind away and hatch the fears
That someday soon the house will die,
No matter how kind folk may try
To keep its life and presence here,
The essence of that day draws near
When all who've lived and dwelt therein,
Though none of them are free from sin
May join their spirits in the strife,
The battle that can save its life,
To stop the builder's endless quest
For redevelopment. The best
That hopeful hearts can hope to do
Is save the place where once there grew
A mansion, built, not just of clay,
But so much more since dawned the day
When first brick placed upon the earth
Gave this mansion of the heart its birth.
Where many have lived and loved there dwells
An aura that surrounds the cells
That help to make a house of peace,
Where love may start and never cease.
And though the years may come and go,
Through summer days and foot-deep snow,
And brick by brick the house may crumble,
Plasters crack and timbers tumble,

Loving care would help it stand
Four-square on its plot of land,
To tell the world – well, all who bother –
Far you'll go to find another
House or home that's been so treated,
Loves well-welcomed, smiles that greeted
Visitors from far afield
Who'd crept along its paths and stealed
Shelter from the world's cruel passion,
Feeling that they'd had their ration
Of the hardships and the pain
Never want to feel again,
Anything but the love and bliss
That might dwell in a house like this.
Long may you stand in empty glory,
No one now may know your story,
Just those echoing waves of sound
That left this mansion, outward bound,
And never human ears shall touch
With wisdom, suffering, knowledge such
As only human hearts have known
But now, out to the stars have flown.

Verses

All I want is a quiet life,
With a cloudless, azure sky,
Where no one thinks to question me,
Or ask me the reason why.

And I can sit and write my verse
With a trouble-free, open mind,
And put my thoughts on paper,
For the benefit of mankind.

My thoughts may not amount to much,
Work at them though I may,
For I have led a simple life,
By year, by month, and day.

With a simple meal and a glass of wine,
I find my verses flow.
But though I write a million words,
I haven't much to show.

My aim is entertainment,
To give a little pleasure;
To show my readers my inner thoughts
That come to me at leisure.

And so, my friends, though late in life,
I struggle to compose,
And hope you may still find some fun,
While the ink in my old pen flows.

Other natural history poetry books by Brambleby Books

Blue Skies in Tuscany – Poems about Life, Love…and Lesser Burdock
Hugh D. Loxdale, ISBN 9780954334727

Bird Words – Poetic Images of Wild birds
Hugh D. Loxdale, ISBN 9780954334734

Up High and Invisible
Keith Davies, ISBN 9780954334758

One under the Sun – A collection of poems
Vincent Spada, ISBN 9780955392863

Love and the Sea
Hugh D. Loxdale, ISBN 9780955392887

The Jena Poems
Hugh D. Loxdale, ISBN 9780955392894

Nevisian Days – Poetry from a Caribbean Isle
Hugh D. Loxdale, ISBN 9781908241009

Bird of Paradise – Selected poems, 1968-2011
Hugh D. Loxdale, ISBN 9781908241016

The Call of the Kokako – Poems from far-flung places
Anthony Boniface, ISBN 9781908241030

Wild Sonnets – Thirty Poems about World Wildlife
Anthony Boniface, ISBN 9781908241207

www.bramblebybooks.co.uk

Follow us on Facebook and Twitter!